AF375234

THE GREATEST GIFT

THE GREATEST GIFT

A POEM BY MOLLIE MORRIS

THE GREATEST GIFT

Published by Happy Self Publishing
www.happyselfpublishing.com
writetous@happyselfpublishing.com

Beautifully Composed in 1982

Illustrated by Sara Morris & Sam Morris

Dedication:

To the glory of God who provided
us so great a salvation.

-Mollie Morris

The season is coming
For trees filled with tinsel
For candles in windows
And glittering stencil

That says, "Merry Christmas!"
Peace, glad tidings!
And carols with echo
Are warm and inviting

A landscaping view
Of houses uneven
Are lighting the sky
With colors in season.

The reds and the greens
The silver and gold
Reminding us of
A story of old.

The story's a babe.
The scene is a stable.
The reason is love.
The bearer, a Savior.

This gift that is fragranced
With love unimagined,
Came wrapped in a package
Of unheard of fashion.

No one would suspect
The king of creation
Could ever be found
In such degradation.

A stable by birth,
And held by a manger,
To most of the world,
This family a stranger.

A donkey and oxen,
And even a lamb,
Yes who would suspect
That even a lamb?

These meager surroundings
Of our little King,
Brought even the praises
Of angels to sing.

This news made it's way
To shepherd's by far.
Their sign from the angels
To follow a star.

14

But God's gracious plan
Was made for the world.
No secrets were kept,
The message unfurled.

Yes, even the evil
Had heard of a king,
That came to deliver
A people to bring.

From bondage to freedom,
From death to new life,
From sickness to health,
And blindness to sight.

This frightened some kings
And princes that heard.
Would their lives be bothered?
Their kingdoms disturbed?

This little boy Jesus
No sooner was born
Brought praises of some,
From others brought scorn.

And growing in wisdom,
He followed His call,
The Father's own business
And baffled them all.

It seemed even though
He was but a youth,
He had an amazing
Grasp of the truth.

Years came and went.
And not much was known
About the boy
From a carpenter's home.

19

Then out from the
Wilderness would appear
A man crying out
For the people to hear.

20

"Make the way ready!
The Lord is at hand!
The one to believe in
Will come in a man!"

"His winnowing fork
Will be his staff.
He's coming to separate
Wheat from the chaff!"

Now Jesus the Man
While 30 or so
Was baptized by John
In the Jordan flow.

And afterwards led
By the Spirit of God,
He came to a place
That was nothing but sod.

And fasting for forty
Days and nights,
He then became hungry
And what came in sight?

But the tempter himself
So full of deceit
Had told Jesus bread
Could be at His feet.

"If you are the Son
Of God, now command
These stones into bread,
Just what you demand."

"No, not bread alone
Could give a man life,
No thing that is eaten
With fork and a knife."

"For true life begins
When man reaches out,
Receiving the Word
From God's holy mouth."

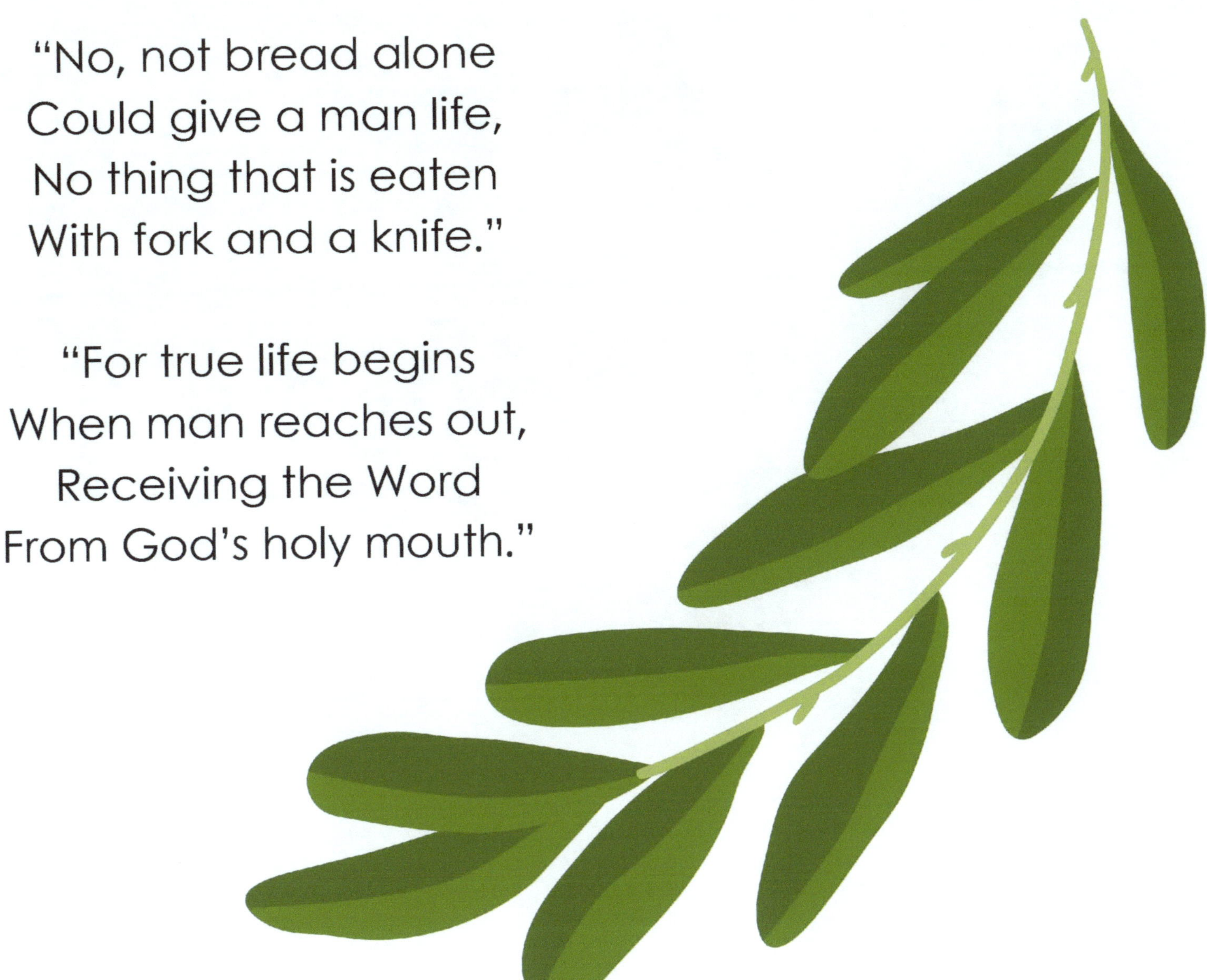

Now Jesus began
To preach to man,
"Repent for the
Kingdom of Heaven's at hand!"

And calling to some,
He said, "Follow Me,
For fisher's of men
Is what you will be."

He spoke to the people
As shepherd to sheep,
The sick and the hungry
Were all at His feet.

Not one was rejected
Whoever had need,
Demand for this teacher
Was great indeed.

He made the lame walk.
Caused the blind to see.
The broken were mended.
What a man was He!

Or was He a man?
No one really knew.
"A prophet!"
Some cried.

"A demon!"
From a few.

"What are we to think
Of this strange Nazarene
Spending most of His time
With people unclean?"

30

"He says that the Sabbath
Was made for man,
And nothing unclean
Was made from God's hand!"

"He's breaking the laws
Our forefathers gave,
"We must stop this man!
Our laws we must save!"

So Pharisees and
Some Sadducees too,
Began testing Him
To see what He would do.

32

But Jesus saw through
Their words and their ways,
Their evil intent
Of what they would say.

Their questions were clever.
And posed to condemn.
He answered them calmly
Silencing them.

This angered them greatly,
Being put to shame
And all the while
He was growing in fame.

"There must be something
This man will say
That will cause the people
To turn in dismay!"

What's this you say?
"You are God's Son?
Redeemer? Savior?
Begotten One?"

"What more needs saying"
He stands condemned!
We must get Pilate
To crucify Him!"

"I see no wrong
This man has done.
You say He calls
Himself God's Son?"

"What have I to do
With your beliefs,
To sentence death
For such as this?"

And seeing the crowd,
Pilate did wish to please.
"There is one way
For Jesus' release."

"No, Give us Barabbas!
And Jesus condemn!"
They cried even louder,
"Crucify Him! Crucify Him!

"Crucify Him!"

"Crucify Him!"

There Jesus hung
Between two thieves.
One of them curses,
The other believes.

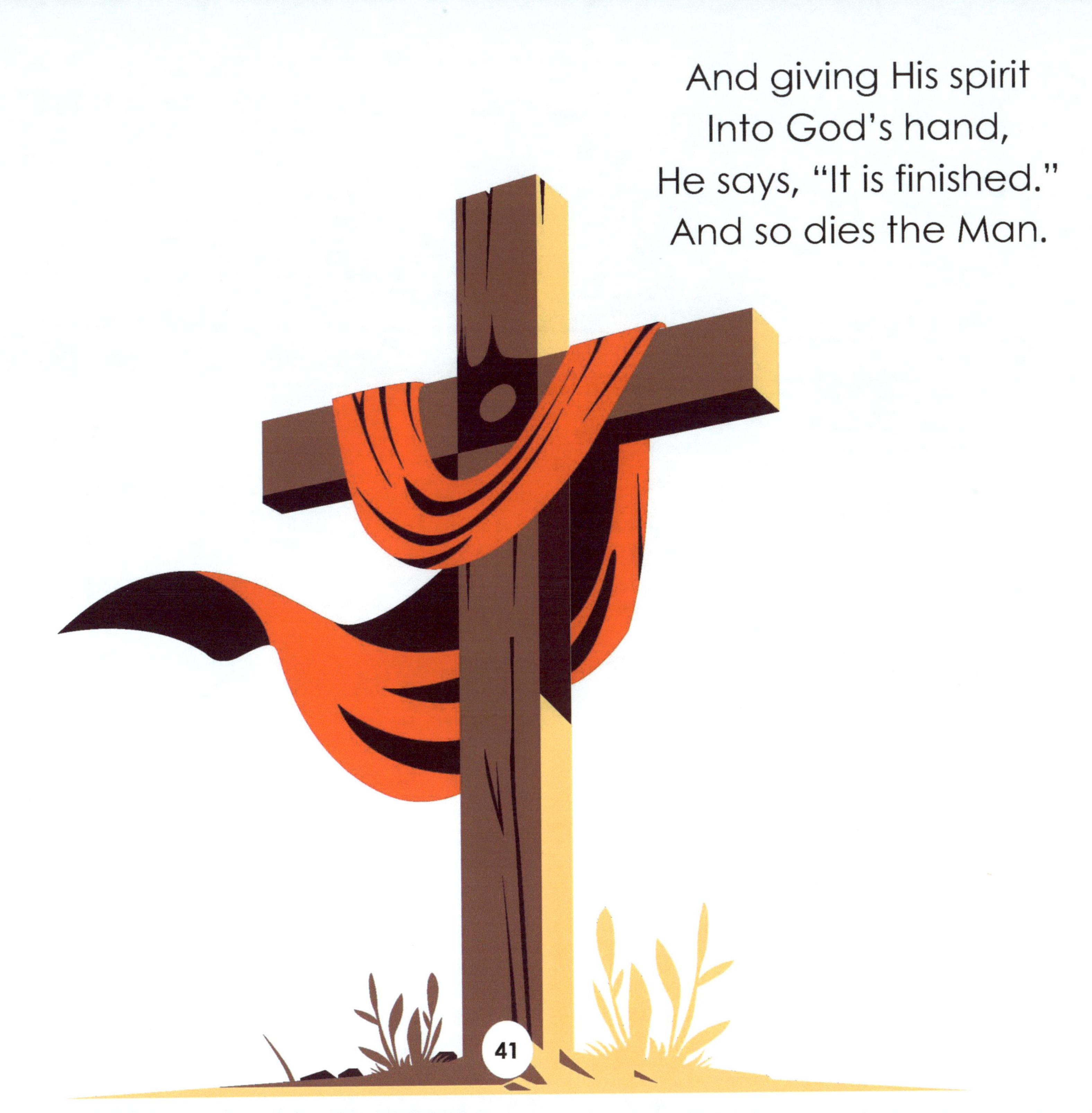

And giving His spirit
Into God's hand,
He says, "It is finished."
And so dies the Man.

No Jesus was not
Just a good man.
He came to die,
To live God's Plan.

Our Savior, Redeemer,
The giver of breath,
Rose victorious,
Conquering death.

For death, there's no victory.
For death, there's no sting.
Jesus is Savior,
Redeemer and King!

He lived and He died,
And He rose again,
Taking the payment
Of sin from man.

So, what will this Christmas
Say to you and to me,
As we plan celebrations
Around Christmas trees?

Will we focus on what
Christ did for man?
The sword in His side?
The nails in His hands?

The rising victorious?
The debt of sin paid?
Eternal life promised?
A way for us made?

I think I will ponder
On Jesus my Lord.
No Christmas gift
Could I ever afford.

He did it for me.
He did it for you.
God's Christmas gift,
Receive it - anew.

The season is coming
For trees filled with tinsel
For candles in windows
And glittering stencil that says,

MERRY CHRISTMAS

Thank You

For reading!

I appreciate all of your feedback, and
I love hearing what you have to say.

Please leave a review on Amazon letting me and
others know what you thought of the book.

Thank you so much!
Mollie Morris

9 798995 201205